Magnificent Objects

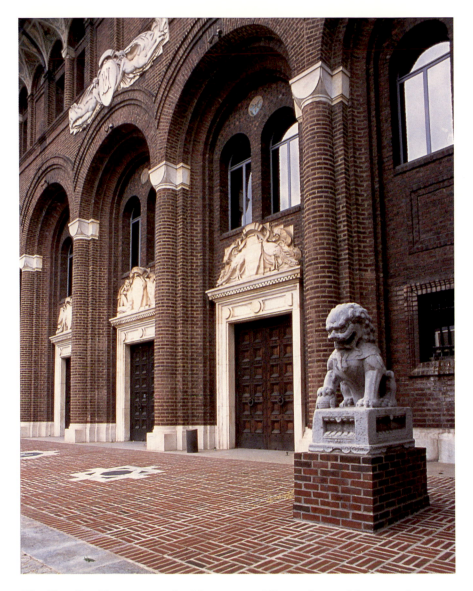

The Trescher Entrance to the University of Pennsylvania Museum of Archaeology and Anthropology.

Magnificent Objects

from the University of Pennsylvania Museum
of Archaeology and Anthropology

Edited by Jennifer Quick

Essay by Deborah I. Olszewski

University of Pennsylvania Museum of Archaeology and Anthropology
Philadelphia

Special thanks to Leroy D. Nunery, Ed.D., Vice President of the Business Services Division, University of Pennsylvania.

Library of Congress Cataloging-in-Publication Data

University of Pennsylvania. Museum of Archaeology and Anthropology.
  Magnificent objects from the University of Pennsylvania Museum of
Archaeology and Anthropology / edited by Jennifer Quick ; essay by
Deborah I. Olszewski ; foreword by John C. Hover II, Sara S. Senior, and
A. Bruce Mainwaring.-- 1st ed.
      p. cm.
Includes index.
  ISBN 1-931707-63-4 (hardcover : alk. paper) -- ISBN 1-931707-64-2
(pbk. : alk. paper)
  1. University of Pennsylvania. Museum of Archaeology and
Anthropology--Catalogs. 2. Ethnological museums and
collections--Pennsylvania--Philadelphia--Catalogs. I. Quick, Jennifer.
II. Title.
  GN36.U62P487 2004
  930.1'074'748--dc22
                                2003025101

Jennifer Quick is Senior Editor in the Publications Department of the University of Pennsylvania Museum of Archaeology and Anthropology.

Printed and bound by Butler and Tanner Ltd., Frome, England.

Contents

Foreword

A book presenting some of the most splendid objects selected from the Museum's vast collections has been a long time in the making. Rather than a guide to a specific gallery, this volume is an appreciation of artifacts from all sections of the Museum. The curators have selected objects for their unique qualities and aesthetic values. The process has been a different kind of endeavor for the research and curatorial staff because they have stepped outside their own disciplines to bring highlights of the Museum to a general readership, bridging worlds, cultures, continents, and time. Each beautiful artifact is represented here in its own right and can serve as a portal to deeper study and appreciation.

Magnificent Objects is also a tribute to Jeremy A. Sabloff's decade of service to the Museum. As the Williams Director, 1994–2004, Dr. Sabloff brought the institution to a new level of achievement. The construction of the Mainwaring Wing for the state-of-the-art storage and maintenance of perishable collections is a most tangible example of his leadership, as is the major renovation and upgrade of the galleries now under way with the essential support of Charles K. Williams II. Jerry's own academic excellence as a Mayanist, theorist, researcher, and teacher is beyond compare. For those who know Jerry Sabloff, in both his personal and his professional demeanor, he is truly a scholar and a gentleman.

The entire Board of Overseers has generously supported and endorsed the publication of this magnificent book, dedicated to Jeremy A. Sabloff. In his tenure as director, he has served with three chairs of the Board. It has been a pleasure and an education for all of us.

John C. Hover II
Chairman, Board of Overseers, 1999– present

Sara S. Senior
Chairman, Board of Overseers, 1996–1999

A. Bruce Mainwaring
Chairman, Board of Overseers, 1991–1995

University of Pennsylvania Museum of Archaeology and Anthropology
Philadelphia
Spring 2004

Board of Overseers 2004

University of Pennsylvania Museum of Archaeology and Anthropology

To

Jeremy A. Sabloff

er holdings. What began as an effort to search for the roots of narratives from the Hebrew Bible yielded unsuspected splendors in the form of burial goods recovered in the Royal Cemetery (Plates 132, 133, 135–138). Justly famous for their delicacy, beauty, and inherent value, these objects in combination with contextual evidence from Ur helped the expedition's leader create an archaeological story of ancient wealth and privilege, especially for the individual identified as Lady Puabi.

Powerful individuals, however, represent only a tiny fraction of humanity's past, which is characterized instead by the nameless multitudes who carried out the day-to-day tasks of life. Hundreds of clay tablets recovered by the joint expedition to Ur partially encapsulate the story of their contributions to society. Many of these are now in the Museum's collections, where, along with the Nippur clay tablets, they serve as a valuable source of data on recipes, finances, religion, mythology, ancient schools, and the minutiae of everyday life in early city-states in the cradle of civilization.

One Sumerian tablet, dating to ca. 1800 BC (Plate 125), tells the story of a legendary flood. Could this early piece of written history be related to the Biblical story of the Flood?

Mesopotamia was not the only area of the world to intrigue both scholars and the public, then and now. The study of ancient Egypt and its civilization from its first dynasties to the Roman period was often made possible through generous donations by patrons. While many of the Egyptian holdings are from excavations sponsored in part by the Museum and obtained under the auspices of its Egypt Exploration Fund, some of the most exciting are the result of fieldwork by Museum scholars. One example is the research at Dendara (see Plate 85) during World War I and afterwards. This site provided copious information about the Middle Kingdom (1980–1630 BC) which greatly expanded knowledge about the revitalization of Egypt after a period of instability.

In addition to its notable Middle Kingdom collections, the Museum also is known for its magnificent New Kingdom (1539–1075 BC) holdings. From Abydos comes a statue of Sitepehu (Plate 95), an overseer of priests who served under Egypt's Queen Hatshepsut; from Herakleopolis, a large seated statue of Ramses II (Plate 88); from Memphis, a relief with the face of a man (Plate 79) from the ceremonial palace of Merenptah, son of Ramses II; and from Thebes, a fragment of the Book of the Dead (Plate 92).

In the early part of the 20th century the Museum also investigated sites in Nubia, where equally important revelations emerged. A stela from Buhen, for example, shows a Kushite ruler as the equivalent of an Egyptian ruler and documents the existence of a significant African kingdom long before the Karanga Kingdom of Great Zimbabwe in sub-Saharan Africa or Jene-Jeno in western Africa. Two statues from Buhen (Plates 78, 86) are examples of people from less regal walks of life. One portrays a Nubian individual whose livelihood was that of the specialized occupation of scribe, while the other is a much lower-ranked person, a gardener. The Museum documented Meroitic culture in excavations at Karanog in Lower Nubia. The characteristic Meroitic painted pottery (Plate 100) and other objects (Plate 98) show the influence of multiple cultures.

Equally important to early and continuing Museum scholarship are the lands and peoples who border on the Mediterranean. As in Mesopotamia, Egypt, and Nubia, the Museum fielded numerous key expeditions that have resulted in unusual discoveries that grace the pages of both scholarly journals and popular media. One of the earliest successes was the 1901 discovery and subsequent excavation of Gournia on Crete, a Minoan Bronze Age settlement. Pottery in the Museum's collections and bronze tools from this site inform us about aspects of the daily life and activities of Minoan people. Other discoveries soon followed, such as Vrokastro, an Early Iron Age site, and Vasiliki, a well-to-do Minoan town made prosperous by its proximity to a good landing spot for ships.

Excavations by Museum staff at the site of Sitio Conte, Panama, documented in meticulous detail the context of the artifacts, which were from unlooted burials from the period between AD 700 and 1100. They recovered large quantities of gold grave offerings, including realistic figures of humans and animals (Plate 38), gold bells, and embossed plaques (Plate 39). We can see the connection of the ethnohistoric present to the more ancient past in the spatial organization of interments in Burial 11 at Sitio Conte. The accounts of the Spanish in Panama in the early 1500s record a society with a three-tiered hierarchy, a societal structure mirroring the three levels of Burial 11, some 400 to 800 years earlier.

Work by the Museum in its early days was not confined to archaeological expeditions. Many of the most exquisite objects are those in the ethnographic and ethnological collections from the Americas, Africa, and Oceania, amply attesting to the accomplishments of indigenous cultures and traditional ways of life. These types of items, dozens of which are shown here (Plates 3, 32, 47, 167, 169, for example), are often unique reminders of the wealth of organic materials rarely recovered during archaeological investigations.

Along with information gathered in the field from living members of many of these cultures, the objects give rare insight into the richness of cultural life in the recent past and, by extension, into the more remote past. Spectacular among the Museum's holdings are Inuit (Eskimo), Northwest Coast (Plates 24, 32), Plains (Plate 26), and Hopi (Plate 27) artifacts, Guatemalan textiles (Plate 43), South American Amazonian featherwork (Plate 50), and items from sub-Saharan Zaire (now the Democratic Republic of Congo; Plates 4, 5, 11, 13, 18, 21) and Sierra Leone (Plate 13), as well as the magnificent artwork from the Kingdom of Benin, one of the greatest of the West African states (Plates 12, 14).

Notable among the Museum's early expeditions to include ethnographic research is the Amazon Expedition from 1913 to 1915. Explorations of the Rio Branco and the Uraricoera tributaries of the Amazon, as well as uncharted forest areas in what today is Guyana, resulted in voluminous records of local cultural practices, hundreds of photographs, and descriptions and measurements of people. Even some archaeological investigation was carried out in caves and on the "island" of Marajo in the mouth of the Amazon. Amazonian headdresses collected during expeditions in the 20th century are particularly striking both physically and culturally. Bird feathers in the Bororo headdress (Plate 50) not only lend beauty to the object, but are believed to represent a type of medicine that enhances the stamina and endurance of the wearer, as well as his fertility.

In other instances, the Museum worked in close association with members of cultural groups to record as much information as possible on the context of each object, including detailed field notes on the oral traditions that are linked to particular images. The impressive collections from the Northwest Coast area made in the first three decades of the 20th century are one example of this collaborative process. A beautiful Tlingit hat (Plate 32) comes from the potlatch ceremony, a type of feast in which food and wealth are given away by the host to the participants. Such ceremonies are an important aspect of cultural life for many groups of Northwest Coast Native Americans.

Early in the Museum's history, holdings were sometimes acquired through purchases, a common practice for museums worldwide in the 19th and early 20th centuries, or through donations. A good number of the African pieces, for example, were acquired in this manner, as well as many of the other ethnographic and ethnological materials from Oceania and the Americas. One particularly outstanding example is a carved wooden chair from Angola (Plate 7). While many of us would barely spare a moment to think of what is now considered an everyday, utilitarian object, chairs often symbolized power and authority. Such is the case for the Angolan chair, carved in the 19th century by a native artisan for a Chokwe chief. It depicts such scenes of everyday life as hunting a baboon and playing a board game (perhaps chess), as well as representing the royal prerogative of the ruler to be seated.

Noteworthy among these already exceptional collections are the objects acquired from the Asian area, in particular, the Buddhist sculptures and paintings, the Chinese Imperial Palace crystal ball (Plate 56), and the stone relief horses of the Emperor Taizong (Plate 57). The adventures of the crystal ball are almost Dickensian: From its original function in Chinese society and as the possession of an infamous dowager empress, it became an exhibit item at the Museum, only to be stolen by vandals in 1988. Fortunately, with the help of the FBI and an observant member of the Museum's staff, it was recovered from the house of a devotee of the occult and put back on display!

Studies by Museum scholars have also concentrated on aspects of human biology, as they can be determined from the examination of skeletal remains. This scientific focus provides details about human variation as it is known during modern and historic times, and is a baseline that can be used to suggest features of prehistoric variability as distant in time as the Paleolithic (Old Stone Age). The Morton collection of human skulls, for example, was made during the early and mid-19th century, and some of its holdings (Plate 179) document aspects of global human variability.

The days of obtaining objects for Museum collections are largely gone, due in part to the establishment of antiquities laws by many countries seeking to retain and preserve their cultural heritage. But Museum scholarship and research have continued with increased vigor. Archaeological expeditions by the Museum in the second half of the 20th and the beginning of the 21st century have included more than 60 forays to such locations as Abydos, Tikal, Vrokastro, Gilund, Hasanlu, Lake Nemi, Kotyiti, Ban Chiang, Corinth, Mongolia, Lake Titicaca, and Pech de l'Azé.

Journey now through storied collections as you peruse in the pages that follow the Museum's magnificent objects of extraordinary splendor. Your travels will mirror the Museum's past and present, as you experience remote antiquity and powerful civilizations, some now extinct, others with vibrant, living descendants.

Magnificent Objects

Sub-Saharan Africa

1. *Beaded Crown* (Ade)

Yoruba people, Eastern Guinea Coast, Nigeria
20th century
Glass beads, cotton base; H. 39.7 cm (15.5 in.)
72-33-1

Among the Yoruba only kings, diviners, and herbalists had the right to wear beaded objects. The *ade* has been in use since the middle of the 17th century and is still worn today on ceremonial occasions by men who can claim descent from Oduduwa, mythical founder and first king of the Yoruba.

The faces on the crown represent various gods from the Yoruba pantheon. Beneath the body of the crown a fringe of beads drapes over the wearer's face, blending the individual's identity with the divine power of the dynasty.

2. *Mask* (Okukwe)

Galwa people, Ogowe River region, Gabon; 20th century
Wood, pigments, feathers; H. without feathers 29.7 cm (11.6 in.)
29-12-188

Masks of this sort identify members of the Okukwe Society, a judicial association. Worn by Okukwe initiates at births, funerals, and initiations, they generally serve to maintain social order by embarrassing guilty individuals in public.

3. *Necklace of Gold Beads*

Asante, Ghana; 19th–20th century
Gold, cotton cord; 36.6 cm (14.3 in.)
70-18-1A–R

Ghana was once called the Gold Coast due to the abundance of the precious metal found in the region. Gold necklaces like this are worn by members of Asante royal families during festivities. The beads are in both abstract and representational forms.

4.   *Neck Rest*

Pende people, Democratic Republic of Congo; late 19th–early 20th century
Wood; H. 17.2 cm (6.7 in.)
AF5154

Neck rests are used throughout West Africa in place of pillows. They
elevate the head to preserve the sleeper's coiffure, an important
element of African dress. The figure has the sharp features and elaborate
scarification characteristic of the Pende.

5. *Female Bowl Bearer* (Mboko)

Luba, Hemba people, Democratic Republic of Congo; 20th century
Wood with iron lancets; H. 32 cm (12.5 in.)
AF5120

Royal diviners use bowl bearers in foretelling and in the investiture of
chiefs. A clay and herb mixture, symbolizing the ancestral spirits, was
kept in the bowl. Diviners applied this paste to their bodies to establish
contact with the spirit world.

6. *Carved Door*

Senufo people, Boundiali region, Ivory Coast; 20th century
Wood, iron; H. 1.65 m (5.4 ft.)
30-10-1

The Senufo indicate wealth and prestige with elaborately carved doors
on clan shrines and the houses of important persons. The designs are
more decorative than religious; however, the animals represent elements
of Senufo cosmology and traditions.

7. *Chief's Chair*

Chokwe, Angola; 19th century
Wood; H. 82.1 cm (32 in.)
62-3-1

Contact with the Portuguese in the 17th century inspired Chokwe artists to carve chiefs' chairs in a European style. This one was embellished with symbols representing the chief's authority. Tableaux from important stages of life appear on the base rails.

8. *Pendant*

Akan, Ivory Coast; 20th century
Gold; Dia. 7.3 cm (2.9 in.)
79-18-1

The king and his court members wear pendants as prestige items. This example, cast by the lost-wax method, depicts a crocodile, one of many animals that symbolize royalty and the strength of the king. The pendants are sometimes attached to staffs, stools, and other ritual regalia.

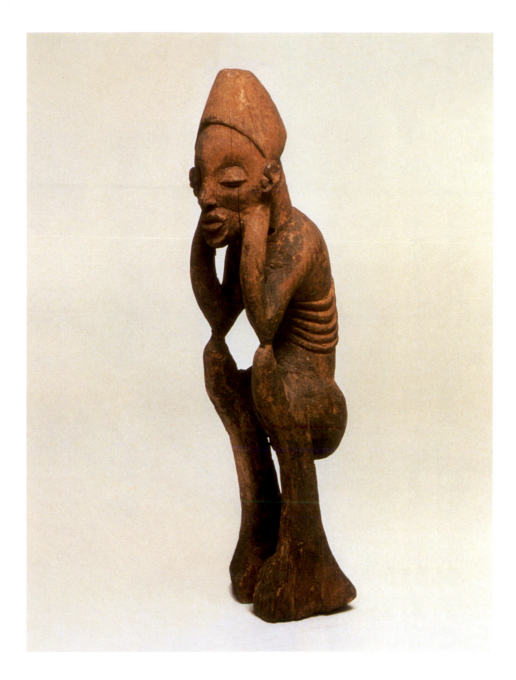

9.   *Female Figure*

Ngala, Angola; 20th century
Wood, traces of pigment; H. 24.6 cm (9.6 in.)
29-59-11

This statuette of a woman with pursed lips, seated in a contemplative
pose, is attributed to the Ngala people, known for their figures
representing primordial ancestors.

10. Silver Necklace

Ethiopia; 20th century
Silver, cotton cord; L. of crescent 20.2 cm (7.9 in.)
87-13-109

Jewelry enhances the beauty and status of the wearer. This large silver necklace, in the shape of a hollow crescent hung on a silver chain, advertised the wealth and taste of its owner. Elaborate beading, incising, and wirework decorate the crescent.

11. Ceramic Jar

Mangbetu people, Democratic Republic of Congo; 19th–20th century
H. 28 cm (11 in.)
AF5360

In the mid-19th century, around the time Belgian colonial rule began,
the Mangbetu began producing pottery featuring women with elaborate
coiffures. The vessels had more of a prestige value than a functional
one and were also given as gifts to foreigners.

12. *Wall Plaque*

Benin Kingdom, Nigeria; 17th–18th century
Brass; H. 41 cm (16 in.)
AF5108

The two figures on this plaque are the king's sacrificers. The one on the left presents the head of an ox. Besides the king, only a few of the highest officials were allowed the privilege of sacrificing oxen to the ancestors.

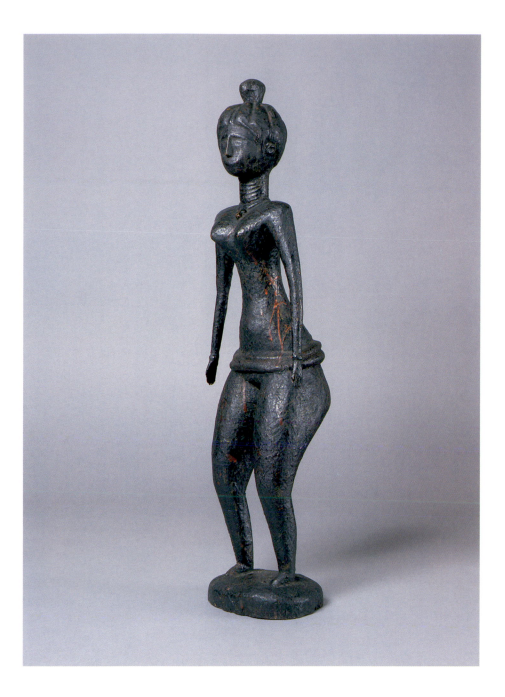

13. *Standing Female Figure*

Temne people, Sierra Leone; 20th century
Wood; H. 56.2 cm (22 in.)
29-94-10

The significance of this figure is not known. Since it is attributed to
the Temne, it may be associated with the initiation of young girls, a
representation of an ideal woman, or a commemorative piece.

14. *Male Reliquary Guardian Figure* (Eyima)

Fang people, Bulu subgroup, Cameroon; 20th century
Wood, inset tooth; H. 59 cm (23 in.)
68-18-1

An important tenet of Fang philosophy stresses balance between the opposing forces that exist in the world and within the individual. Reliquary figures and masks often reflect this ideal. The carvings guard ancestral bones from antisocial elements.

15. *Woman Holding Child*

Baule, Ivory Coast; 20th century
Wood, metal studs; H. 44.5 cm (17.4 in.)
29-12-68

This sculpture represents either a spirit wife or nature spirit. The Baule believe every person has a spirit spouse, revealed in dreams, who is responsible for the problems in their lives. The nature spirit grants fruitful harvest and hunts if properly honored.

16. Dance Clappers with Birds of Prophecy

Benin Kingdom, Nigeria; 17th–18th century
Brass; H. (l.) 31 cm (12 in.), (r.) 33.5 cm (13 in.)
AF5085, AF2048

Chiefs carry clappers during the Ọrọ festival, dancing with them and beating the bird's beak in remembrance of the prophetic bird killed by a certain chief because it prophesied his defeat in war.

17. *Double Armlet*

Yoruba people, Owo region, Nigeria; 19th–20th century
Ivory; H. 10.5 cm (4.1 in.)
29-93-5

This armlet consists of two interlocking cylinders made from the same tusk and carved with figures in low relief. Because bird and serpent figures denote rank in Yoruba culture, royalty and nobility wear such armlets to proclaim their authority.

18. *Dance Staff* (Thafu Malwangu)

Kongo, Yombe people, Democratic Republic of Congo; 20th century
Wood, raffia, kaolin, seed pods; H. 55 cm (21.5 in.)
AF35

The leader of a boys' initiation society carried this staff in dances that taught the beliefs of the community. The figures seated back to back may be the mythical twins Makuala and Matundu, who are spirits of a rainbow cult.

19. Carved Staffs

Ovimbundu (l.) and Songo (c. and r.) peoples, Angola; 20th century
Wood; iron, brass, tin (c.); orange pigment (r.). H. (l. to r.) 76.5 cm (29.8 in.),
87 cm (33.9 in.), 60.7 cm (23.7 in.)
29-59-169, 29-59-207, 29-59-181

Kings, chiefs, and other men of importance carried staffs such as these
to announce their rank in society. They often turned these staffs, along
with other regalia, over to the succeeding ruler.

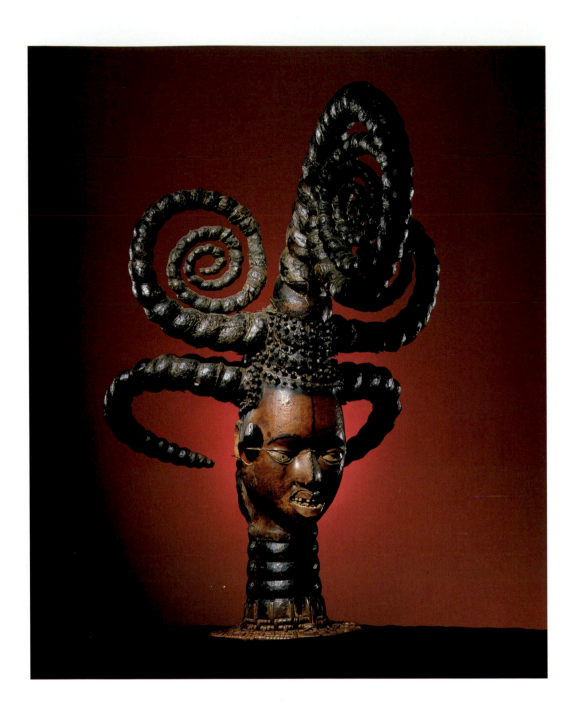

20. *Nsikpe Dance Crest*

Ejagham, Calabar, Nigeria; 20th century
Wood, antelope skin, basketry, iron nails; H. 69 cm (27 in.)
82-1-1

Skin-covered masks with coiffures of spiral braids are characteristic of communities in the Cross River region of Nigeria and Cameroon. Members of various societies, such as the Nsikpe, wear the masks on special occasions to enforce laws and maintain peace.

21. *Mask* (Mbuya)

Pende people, Democratic Republic of Congo; 20th century
Wood, pigment, raffia cloth, raffia; H. 57.5 cm (22.4 in.)
77-4-1

Young Pende wore masks like this in performances at the end of
initiation ceremonies to demonstrate their knowledge of the values and
customs of Pende society. Since the 1930s the entertainment aspects of
the performances have predominated.

22. *Reliquary Guardian Figure* (Mbulu Ngulu)

Kota, Mindassa-Bawumbu people, Gabon/Congo; 20th century
Wood, copper, brass, iron; H. 48 cm (18.7 in.)
29-12-227

Guardian figures are placed on baskets containing the bones of
ancestors to ward off evil forces. The relics and their guardians are kept
in the houses of family heads, and offerings are made to them to bring
fertility, success in hunting, health, and prosperity.

23. *Standing Female Figure*

Baga, Guinea Bissau; 20th century
Wood, glass beads; H. 47.6 cm (18.6 in.)
29-12-92

Male or female figures of this type represent deities that had potentially both good and evil influence over the life of communities. Kept in shrines outside the villages, they served as intermediaries between the spirit and the earthly worlds.

North
America

24. Oyster Catcher Rattle

Tlingit, Chilkat, Alaska
Ca. AD 1890
Wood, pigment, ermine fur, hair, hide; L. 37 cm (14.4 in.)
NA4972

This type of rattle was commonly used by Tlingit shamans to attract the attention and support of their helping spirits. The rattle depicts an oyster catcher, a large and elegant crane of the region. On its back and within a bear-shaped boat sit a shaman and another figure, possibly his patient.

25. *Red Mesa Black-on-white Bowl*

Ancestral Pueblo, Red Mesa, northeastern Arizona; ca. AD 870–950
Clay, mineral pigment; Dia. 21 cm (8.2 in.)
29-77-422

Like many prehistoric Pueblo bowls, the painted interior of this
example includes four design elements around a central rectangle and
conveys a strong sense of motion and energy. The design may refer to
the four quarters of the world.

26. *Painted Parfleche*

Northern Plains, Blackfeet (Blood); ca. 1885
Rawhide, pigment; W. 35.9 cm (14 in.)
29-47-184

Parfleche containers were commonly used by 19th century Plains, Plateau, and Southwestern nomadic peoples to store and transport personal items and food. The bags were easily tied onto a saddle and carried on horseback. The design may portray animal or cosmic imagery.

27. *Monster Woman* (Soyok Wuhti) *Katsina*

Hopi, Arizona; late 19th century
Cottonwood, feathers, hair; 25.4 cm (9.9 in.)
38870

Katsinas are Pueblo spirit messengers who live in the sacred San Francisco Peaks. Monster Woman, a terrifying katsina with red hair, visits Hopi villages in the spring. She wanders from house to house, hooting in a shrill voice, demanding that children eat what they are served.

28. Root Clubs

Penobscot, Maine; ca. 1875
Painted wood; L. of larger 71.5 cm (27.9 in.)
L-84-2123, L-84-2124

In the mid-19th century, Penobscot, Passamaquoddy, and other Wabanaki native carvers in Maine began to sell root clubs—once used in battle and as symbols of office—to tourists. With this outside interest, carvers added color and human faces to the clubs.

29. *Man's Shoulder Bag*

Jerry Ingram, Louisiana Choctaw; 2002
Wool, cotton, glass beads, cotton thread; W. of pouch 19 cm (7.4 in.)
2002-9-2

Choctaw artist Jerry Ingram created this shoulder bag which is similar to those made by his ancestors in the 18th and 19th centuries. Ingram is concerned with revitalizing the old styles of material culture through his ongoing study of Choctaw collections in museums.

30. Beaded Man's Leggings

Menomini, Wisconsin; ca. 1890
Velvet cloth, glass beads; L. 71 cm (27.7 in.)
NA5389

After contact, native women of the Great Lakes region changed their traditions of dress regalia, incorporating European-inspired embroidery techniques, floral designs, and materials. These velvet leggings depict bud and blossom designs made with glass trade beads.

31. *Ceremonial Pipe*

Lakota, South Dakota; ca. 1890
Catlinite; L. of stem 38.5 cm (15 in.)
L-84-1391a,b

Native Americans made pipes in a variety of materials, but favored catlinite. Traditionally, the red stone is said to represent the blood of their
people. Pipes were carved for important occasions, trade, and religious
purposes. This example, with plant designs, was made for sale to tourists.

32. *"Raven Barbecuing" Hat*

Tlingit, L'ookna̱x.ádi Clan, Sea Lion House, Sitka, Alaska; ca. AD 1800–1900
Wood, pigment, ermine, puffin beaks, hide; H. 50 cm (19.5 in.)
NA8502

For Tlingit people, objects frequently embody individual and clan histories and are the subjects of historical narratives. Here the hat depicts Raven, an important Tlingit moiety emblem, in an episode in which he kills and greedily eats the king salmon.

33. *Beaded Basket*

Pomo, northern California; ca. 1890
Willow, glass beads, abalone shell; Dia. (greatest) 23 cm (9 in.)
NA7890

At the turn of the 20th century, Pomo women scaled down the size of their traditional baskets to meet the lucrative demands of the tourist market. This evenly coiled, colorful example is decorated with glass trade beads and abalone shell.

34. *Man's Poncho-Serape*

Navajo, Arizona; ca. 1850
Wool, indigo (blue), cochineal, and lac (red) dyes; L. 176.5 cm (69.5 in.)
76-23-1

Taught to weave by the Pueblo, Navajo women, and increasingly men,
have maintained a strong hand-weaving tradition for more than 350 years.
This poncho-serape exemplifies Navajo woven clothing and design before
the dramatic influences of the tourist trade that began in the 1890s.

Mesoamerica

35. *Pottery Whistle*

Central Veracruz, Mexico
Ca. AD 800
H. 11.5 cm (4.5 in.)
69-24-1

This clay whistle depicts a woman in elaborate dress. Although clothing from ancient Mexico rarely survives, pre-Columbian figurines such as this provide tantalizing hints of the intricate weaves and embroidered patterns of ancient Mexican textiles.

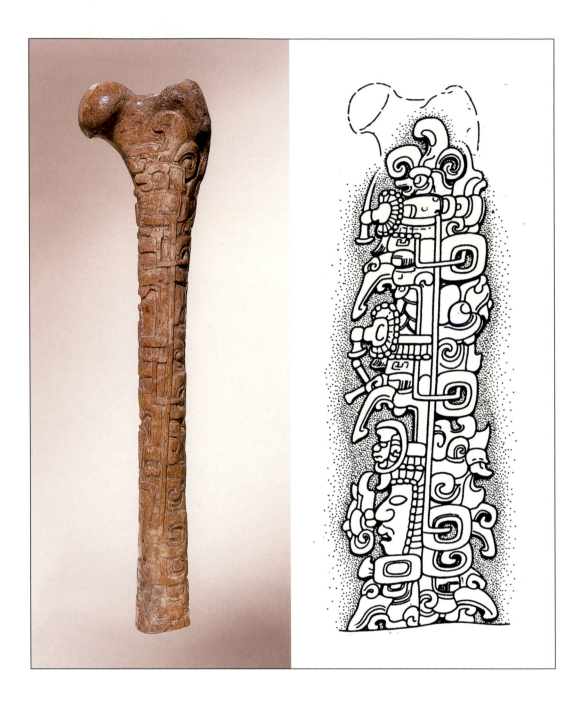

36. Carved Bone and Drawing of Design

Maya, Guatemala; AD 400
Animal bone; L. 21 cm (8.2 in.)
68-32-2b

This and other bones were recovered from a tomb in western Mexico's
Michoacan region, yet they are carved in the Early Classic style of
Tikal, Guatemala, a Maya site located 500 miles to the east.

37. *Vase, with Rollout Painting (detail)*

Maya, Chamá, Guatemala; AD 700–900
Clay; H. 23.5 cm (9.2 in.)
38-14-1. Painting: T4-2618

The two principal figures in this scene are painted black, the color associated with the Maya god of merchants. The man in the jaguar-skin cape may be a chief or shaman. This is one of a series of paintings of Maya pottery made by Mary Louise Baker, the Museum's resident artist, in 1938.

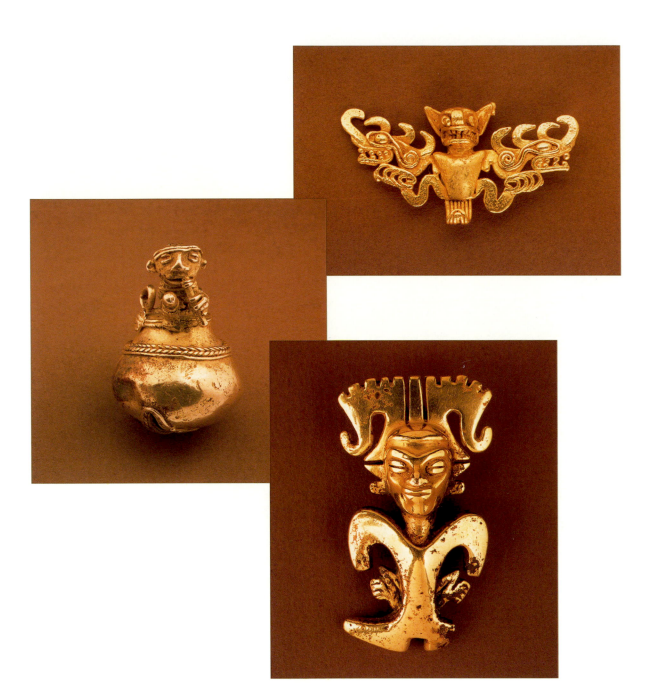

38. *Bat, Bell, and Human Pendants*

Coclé, Sitio Conte, Panama; ca. AD 700–900
Gold; H. of human figure 5.8 cm (2.3 in.)
40-13-33, 40-13-198, 40-13-28

Made using the lost-wax casting technique, these pendants were recovered during University of Pennsylvania Museum–sponsored excavations at Sitio Conte. They were found with an abundance of other gold ornaments in Coclé elite human burials.

39. *Plaque*

Coclé, Sitio Conte, Panama; ca. AD 700–900
Gold; H. 20.6 cm (8 in.)
40-13-2

This plaque was attached to the clothing of a high-ranking individual. Sixteenth century Spanish accounts reveal that paramount chiefs from the region were entitled to wear gold plaques in war and in death. The anthropomorphized birds probably represent a Coclé mythic figure.

40. "Smiling Face" Mask

Remojadas, Veracruz, Mexico; AD 500–700
Clay; H. 15.5 cm (6 in.)
61-1-1

Masks and figurines with smiling faces are typical of the Remojadas
culture. Most were not excavated systematically and their function is
still uncertain. Many scholars believe they were for ritual purposes, and
the facial expression may indicate a hallucinogen-induced trance state.

41. Pendants

Maya, Guatemala?; AD 600–900
Jadeite; H. (l.) 5.7 cm (2.2 in.), (r.) 5.5 cm (2.15 in.)
NA5897, NA5900

Jadeite was highly prized by the Maya and was fashioned into pendants, necklaces, earrings, and plaques. Found in Mexico, these pendants may be true portraits of Maya lords. They wear earplugs, necklaces, and elaborate headdresses.

42. Ear Ornaments

Jalisco, Mexico; ca. AD 1300–1500
Turquoise, wood, wax; H. (top piece) 5.2 cm (2 in.)
NA5194

The use of turquoise in mosaic adornments was highly prized by the Aztecs, who valued the workmanship of the craftsmen of West Mexico and required turquoise jewelry and masks as tribute items.

43. *Embroidered* Huipil

Santa Maria Nebaj, Department of El Quiche, Guatemala; 1960s style
Cotton; L. (shoulder to hem) 68 cm (26.5 in.)
84-27-1

This woman's blouse was typical attire in the Mayan community of
Santa Maria Nebaj in the 1960s. Woven on a back-strap loom, it is
constructed of two warp-faced panels of cotton with colorful supple-
mentary weft designs depicting animals, plants, and human figures.

South America

44. Gold Lime Container

Quimbaya, Colombia
Probably Early Quimbaya, 200 BC–AD 1000
H. 23 cm (9 in.)
SA 2751

This gold container from Colombia was probably used to hold powdered lime, which was mixed with crushed coca leaves and chewed by elite Andean individuals. The mixture acted as a mild stimulant in the cold, high-altitude environment. The hollow flask is also a rattle and depicts a young female figure with closed eyes, wearing nose, ear, neck, knee, and ankle ornaments. She holds a young plant in each hand.

45. *Poncho*

Paracas Peninsula, southern coast of Peru; ca. 450–175 BC
Cotton and camelid fibers; L. 74.4 cm (29 in.)
SA4604

Weaving and embroidery were specialty crafts of paramount importance in Paracas, an agricultural and fishing community. This small poncho with embroidered border was worn as ritual attire, most likely by an elite individual. The colorful design depicts large and small birds, probably condors.

46. *Ceremonial* Kero

Inca, Peru; Colonial Period, ca. AD 1550
Wood, pigment, plant resin; H. 20.5 cm (8 in.)
43531

Inca rulers presented *keros*, drinking cups for maize beer, to their conquered subjects as a sign of their dominance and control. After Spanish rule, *keros* became symbols of indigenous identity. This example, reflecting European influence, depicts an Inca chief in typical dress, holding his staff of office.

47. *Andean Textile Fragment*

North Coast, Peru; ca. AD 1000–1476
Wool, camelid fiber; W. 35 cm (13.7 in.)
CG 852611-6459

The vast numbers of textiles recovered from burials in Peru's coastal desert
reveal complex weaving techniques and sophisticated dyeing methods.
There, cloth has long been a medium of symbolic expression and exchange.
In this fragment, animals, fish, and birds surround the central figure.

48. *Gold Breastplate*

Antioquia, Colombia; ca. AD 600–1000
W. 55 cm (21.5 in.)
SA2702

This breastplate was found in the burial mound of a powerful Sinú chief in the tropical Andean region of Ayapel. It was with a large number of other gold funerary offerings, which together reaffirmed the political and ritual prestige of this individual.

49. *Silver Beaker*

Chimu, north coast of Peru; ca. AD 1000–1476
H. 41 cm (16 in.)
SA4611

This container, depicting a raptor-like figure with a large beak, may have been used to serve maize beer. There are two raised ears of maize at the back of the head, and three rows of maize kernels encircle the crown. In Peru, where potatoes are a staple crop, maize is considered a delicacy.

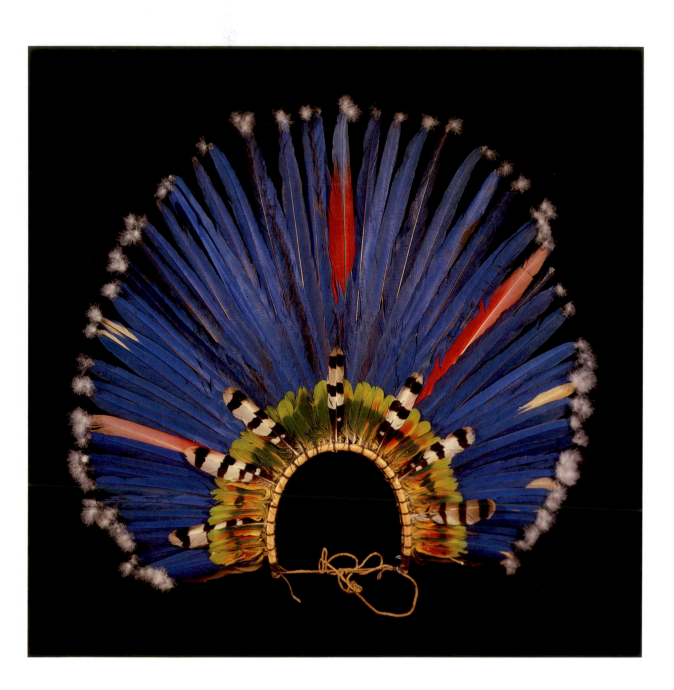

50. *Feather Headdress*

Bororo, Brazil; ca. 1920
Macaw and harpy eagle feathers, plant fiber; H. 48.7 cm (19 in.)
CG2003-2-1

For the Bororo of central Brazil, feather decorations distinguish their superiority over animals and other humans and represent social rank within lineages. The spirit of each macaw species belongs to a single clan whose members wear ornaments made of that bird's feathers.

51. *Vessel in the Shape of a Warrior*

Moche, Peru; ca. AD 150–700
Clay; H. 25.6 cm (10 in.)
39-20-70

Ceramics made by the Moche are renowned for their realistic portraiture and complex scenes. This stirrup-spout jar depicts an elite warrior-priest wearing ear spools, tunic, an elaborate helmet, and shield and holding a massive stone club. Such vessels were placed as offerings in burial tombs.

52. *Silver Pins*

Mapuche, Chile; ca. 1860
L. of longest pin 34.6 cm (13.5 in.)
SA4560, SA1077, SA4559, SA4699

The traditional garb of 19th century Mapuche women included elaborate silver pins worn at the neck to attach a handwoven woolen shoulder blanket. Such ornaments have magical qualities: for the Mapuche, silver represents the tears of the moon released in an argument with the sun.

53. *Votive Figure of a Woman*

Inca, Peru; ca. AD 1476–1550
Silver; H. 23 cm (9 in.)
SA2490

This hollow silver votive was probably paired with a gold figure and offered at a human burial as a gift to the sun or in a sacred place to a spirit being. It was most likely not intended to be viewed as shown, but would have been dressed in miniature woven garments at the time of its use.

54. *Bottle* (Urpu)

Inca, Temple of the Sun, Pachacamac, Peru; ca. AD 1476–1550
Clay; H. 33.3 cm (13 in.)
31017

Bottles of this shape held maize beer at Inca feasts and ritual occasions. This example was probably presented as a royal gift or offering. The concentric diamond design indicates it was made in Cuzco, rather than at the ceremonial center of Pachacamac 300 miles to the west where it was found.

55. Statue of Guanyin

China
Jin Dynasty (AD 1115–1234)
Wood
H. 2.14 m (7 ft.)
C408

Guanyin is the Chinese name of the bodhisattva of compassion and mercy. This statue has several layers of color, indicating that it has been repainted a number of times. This would have earned merit for the restorers, as well as improved the appearance of the statue.

56. *Crystal Ball on Silver Stand*

China; Qing Dynasty (AD 1644–1911)
Quartz crystal, silver; Dia. of ball 25.4 cm (10 in.)
C681A, B

The ball of Burmese crystal may have been made for the Empress Dowager Cixi, and is thought to be the second-largest crystal ball in the world. The silver stand in the shape of a wave was designed by a Japanese artist.

57. One of the Horses of Tang Taizong

China; Tang Dynasty (AD 618–906)
Limestone; H. 1.73 m (5.7 ft.)
C395

Emperor Taizong ordered six stone panels for his mausoleum carved with images of his favorite horses. The horse on this particular relief has been identified as "Autumn Dew"; Taizong's general is removing an arrow from the animal's chest.

62. *Seated Sakyamuni in Meditation*

China; Yuan Dynasty (AD 1271–1368)
Gilded wood; H. 81 cm (32 in.)
C405

Sakyamuni is a name given to the historical Buddha, Gautama
Siddhartha, the founder of Buddhism. Five Buddhist sutras were found
inside the statue; four were in Chinese and one was in Tibetan.

63. *Camel Mortuary Figure*

China; Tang Dynasty (AD 618–906)
Clay with glaze; H. ca. 92.4 cm (36 in.)
C466

The Tang dynasty is known for its tricolored tomb figurines, especially those depicting foreign animals and figures. Horses and camels, including camels carrying musicians, are especially common.

66. *Luohan in a Pose of Meditation*

China; Liao-Jin Dynasty (ca. 11th century AD)
Clay with tricolor glaze; H. 1.21 m (3.9 ft.), including stand
C66A,B

Luohan are monks, disciples of the Buddha Sakyamuni. They often
travel and are depicted in groups of sixteen, eighteen, or even five hun-
dred. This luohan, perhaps a portrait of an individual monk, wears a
jiasa, or patchwork robe.

67. *Seated Patriarch or Monk*

Japan; 18th–19th century
Wood, paint, lacquer; H. of chair 84 cm (32.8 in.)
29-96-338, 29-96-339

Zen Buddhism was transmitted to Japan from China. It became popular
in the late 12th and early 13th centuries. This life-sized painted and
lacquered figure may be a portrait of a highly respected monk.

78. *Statue of the Scribe Amenemhat*

Buhen, Lower Nubia
Reign of Hatshepsut, Dynasty 18, ca. 1460 BC
Diorite; H. 37 cm (14.4 in.)
E10980

Amenemhat was an Egyptianized Nubian who worked in the Egyptian administration of the 18th Dynasty, when the female pharaoh Hatshepsut ruled. This statue comes from the fortress-town of Buhen and is one of the fine examples of statuary uncovered by the Museum's Coxe Expedition.

79. *Relief of a Man*

Memphis (Mit Rahina), Egypt; Dynasty 26? (664–525 BC)
Limestone; H. 20 cm (7.8 in.)
E13643

The figure is carved in sunk relief, while the features of the head, especially details of the ear, are raised. Although the findspot, the palace of King Merenptah, as well as details suggest a possible date in the Ramesside Period, the overall style and some features favor a later period.

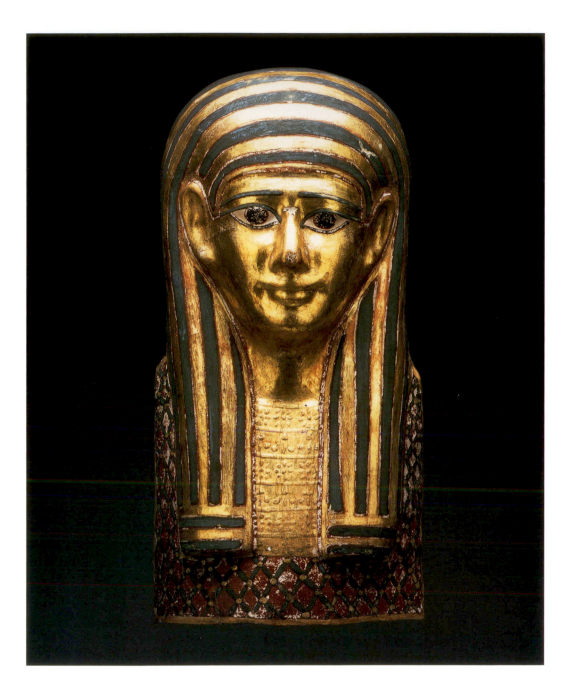

80. *Gilded Mask*

Provenience unknown; Ptolemaic-Roman Period (after 300 BC)
Gilded cartonnage; H. 52.1 cm (20.5 in.)
53-20-1a

This mask originally covered the head of a mummy. The deceased, in a long wig, is shown in an idealized fashion. The golden flesh may represent the skin of the immortal Egyptian gods. The mask is made of plaster-soaked linen molded into shape, hardened, then painted.

81. *Gold Sekhmet Necklace*

Memphis (Mit Rahina), Egypt; Dynasty 26, reign of Amasis (570–526 BC)
Gold and chalcedony; H. of amulet 7.6 cm (3 in.)
29-70-19

This necklace consists of cowrie shell–shaped beads, two large barrel-shaped beads, a pomegranate-shaped bead, and a cast solid gold amulet of the goddess Sekhmet. Depicted as a woman with the head of a lioness, Sekhmet was the consort of Ptah, the patron deity of the Memphite area.

82. *Shabti*

Possibly from Deir el Medina, Egypt; Dynasty 19 (1292–1190 BC)
Wood, pigment; H. 23.6 cm (9.2 in.)
E12615a

Shabtis were found in tombs from the Middle Kingdom onward. Their purpose was to perform the work the deceased was called to do in the afterworld. This is a shabti of the Lady Maya.

Mediterranean

101. *Attic Red-figure Pyxis (Cosmetic Container)*

By the Meleager Painter
Ca. 400–390 BC
Terracotta; Dia. 21.8 cm (8.6 in.)
MS5462

The lid of the pyxis depicts Heracles and Hebe's wedding in the presence of the gods on Mt. Olympus. Heracles holds Hebe by the hand, while a goddess lights the scene with a pair of torches. Athena and Zeus sit enthroned, while Hera leans intimately against Zeus's shoulder in the presence of various Eros or Cupid figures. Two women carry a jewel box for the bride and a vessel containing water for her bridal bath.

102. *Gold Necklace*

Provenience unknown; Etruria, Italy; 4th century BC
L. 34 cm (13.4 in.)
MS4021

The design of elaborate necklaces like this derived from Phoenician types and also appeared in Orientalizing Greek jewelry. Interspersed with spacers are pendants in the shape of grape clusters, bullae (discs), and vases from which female heads emerge.

103. *Roman Perfume Bottle* (Unguentarium)

Syria; mid-1st century AD
Glass; H. 16.7 cm (6.6 in.)
MS5005

Many of the *unguentaria* of the 1st century AD were mass produced.
Occasionally, however, a vessel like this one stands out because of its
delicacy of shape and color. A white spiral was one of the most fashion-
able decorative motifs for smaller items of glassware.

104. *Roman Burial* Loculus *Cover (detail)*

Provenience unknown; late 2nd–3rd century AD
Marble; L. 175 cm (69 in.)
MS4017

While the scene of the triumphal procession of the god Bacchus and his
merry entourage is closely related to those on the front of many
sarcophagi, this relief seems to have been made as a single panel to
cover a burial niche in a tomb chamber.

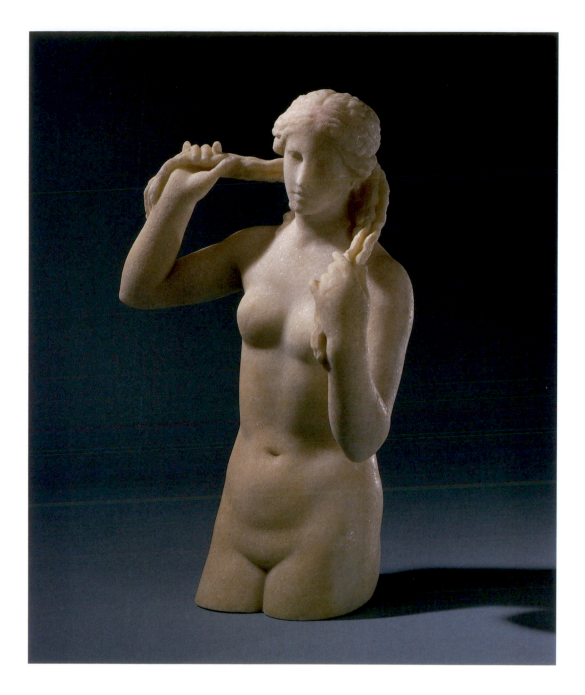

105. *"Benghazi Venus"*

Benghazi, Libya; late 2nd–1st century BC
Marble; H. 32 cm (12.6 in.)
69-14-1

In this Hellenistic statuette of Aphrodite Anadyomene ("Rising from the Sea"), the goddess of love emerges from the waves, wringing the salt water from her hair. This was one of the most popular subjects in Greek sculpture.

106. *Etruscan Antefix (Roof Ornament)*

Caere (Cerveteri), Italy; later 4th century BC
Terracotta; H. 26.5 cm (10.4 in.)
MS1801

This woman wears horseshoe-shaped earrings, a torque necklace, and a
large diadem. The use of hatching to create contours and shading,
together with the delicate pastels and muted tones of the colors, recall
4th century painted tombs.

107. *Pair of Hellenistic Gold Earrings*

Cyprus; late 4th–2nd century BC
Dia. 2.1 cm (0.8 in.) (shown about actual size in inset)
34-1-1

Each earring takes the form of a bull's head and neck. Jewelry making use of animals (lions, gazelles, griffins) became widely popular during this period. Jewelry is frequently represented in scenes on vases and sculptures.

108. Scythian Panther Head and Stag Plaques

Maikop, Kuban River region, south Russia; 5th century BC
Gold; (l.) 2.5 cm (1.0 in.), (r.) 5.0 cm (2.0 in.)
30-33-1, 30-33-2A

The Scythians, a nomadic people living north of the Black Sea in the 1st millennium BC, are famous for the use of animal forms in their arts and for their lavish royal burials replete with gold artifacts. These appliqué plaques, part of a group, were probably once sewn to a shirt.

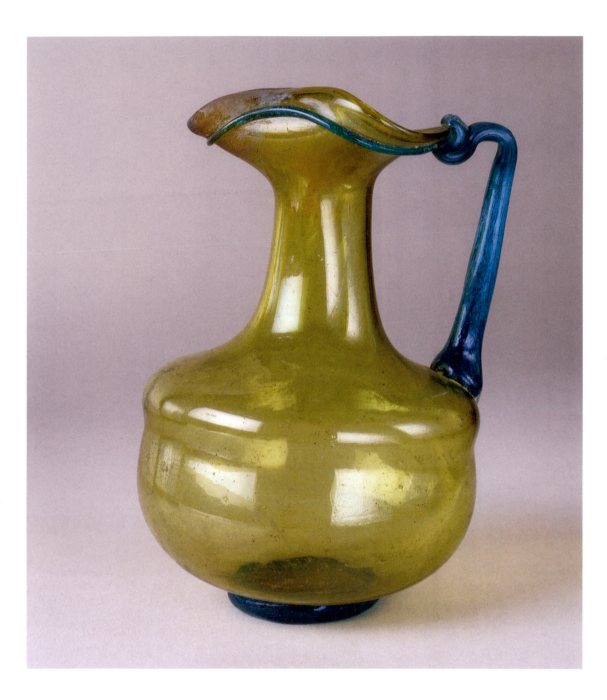

109. Roman Squat Glass Jug

Probably from Aleppo, Syria; 4th century AD
H. 12.8 cm (5 in.)
MS5134. Digital image courtesy of Stuart Fleming

The combination of colors on this vessel—amber for the body,
turquoise for the handle—and the single coil decoration applied around
the rim were particularly popular for glassware of this period.

110. *Roman Relief Plaque with Masks*

Sanctuary of Diana Nemorensis, Lake Nemi, Italy; 1st century AD
Marble; L. 44 cm (17.3 in.)
MS3459

With masks of Pan, god of the countryside, and a youthful Dionysos, god of wine, this type of relief was appropriate for use in a Roman theater or as a garden decoration. The plaque shown here probably decorated the small theater in the Sanctuary of Diana at Lake Nemi.

111. *Attic Red-figure Stamnos*

By the Kleophrades Painter; ca. 490 BC
Terracotta; H. 33.5 cm (13.2 in.)
L-64-185 (on loan, Philadelphia Museum of Art)

Heracles is shown fighting the ferocious Nemean Lion. After ruining all his weapons on the creature's impervious hide, Heracles resorted to choking it to death. Afterwards he wore its skull as a helmet and its skin for a cloak.

112. Gems from the Maxwell Sommerville Collection

Left: Post-Antique onyx cameo featuring the portrait of a noblewoman of the Italian Renaissance, with elaborately styled hair.
Provenience unknown; 16th century. L. 4.9 cm (1.9 in.). 29-128-63

Top center: Roman banded agate seal in modern ring setting; a female figure, perhaps a maenad or the goddess Venus, is shown dancing.
Carved in Italy; 1st–2nd century BC. L. 1.4 cm (0.6 in.). 29-128-552

Top right: Roman carnelian intaglio in modern ring setting shows Apollo holding a laurel branch and his sister, Artemis, with her bow.
Provenience unknown; 2nd–3rd century AD. L. 1.7 cm (0.7 in.). 29-128-904

Bottom center: Post-Antique carnelian seal set as a gold pendant depicting Demeter-Ceres, the goddess of the harvest, wearing a wreath of grain.
Carved in Rome or Vienna; 18th century. L. 2.2 cm (0.9 in.). 29-128-879

Bottom right: Roman carnelian stamp seal in modern ring setting. A bearded soldier dressed in armor holds a sacrificial dish over an altar.
Carved in Italy; 2nd century BC. L. 2.2 cm (0.9 in.). 29-128-900

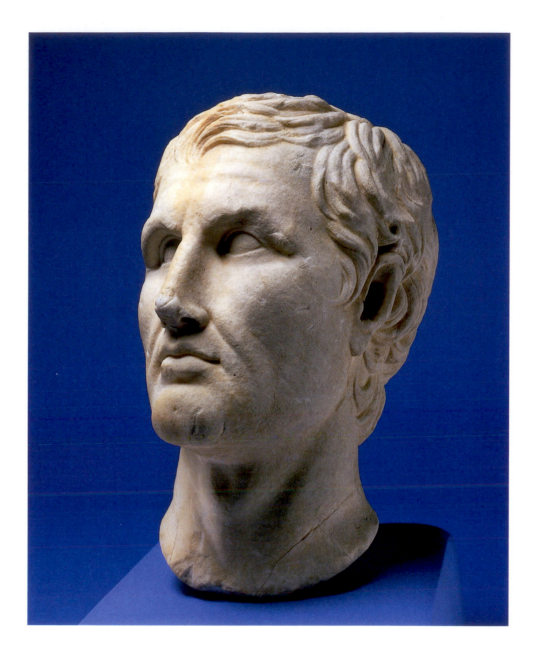

113. *Hellenistic Portrait of Menander*

Montecelio, Italy; mid-1st century AD after early 3rd century BC Greek original
Marble; H. 34.5 cm (13.6 in.)
MS4028

Menander (ca. 342–291 BC) was the outstanding Athenian comic play-
wright of his era. This is one of more than sixty Roman copies, all pre-
sumably adapted from an original bronze seated statue erected in the
Theater of Dionysos in Athens.

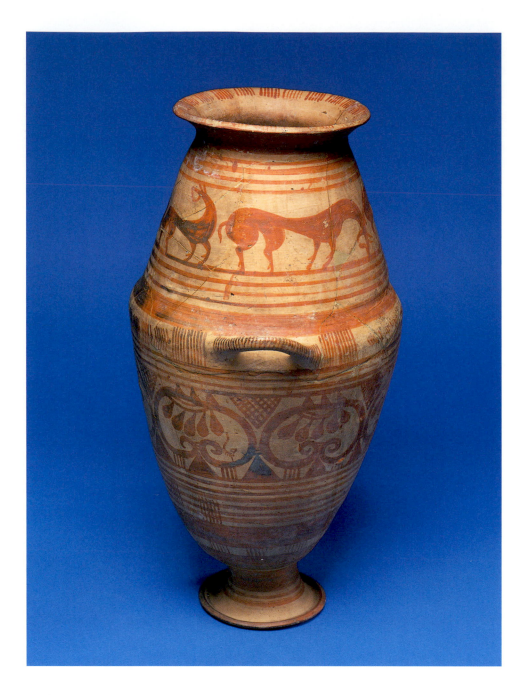

114. *Etruscan/Faliscan Red-on-white Painted Urn*

Narce, Tomb 1, Italy; 7th century BC
Terracotta; H. 48.3 cm (19.0 in.)
MS2730

With its curvilinear patterns and stylized animals, this ceramic urn is representative of the lush images of Etruscan art derived from Greek and Phoenician exchange. The vase shape, however, is native Etruscan.

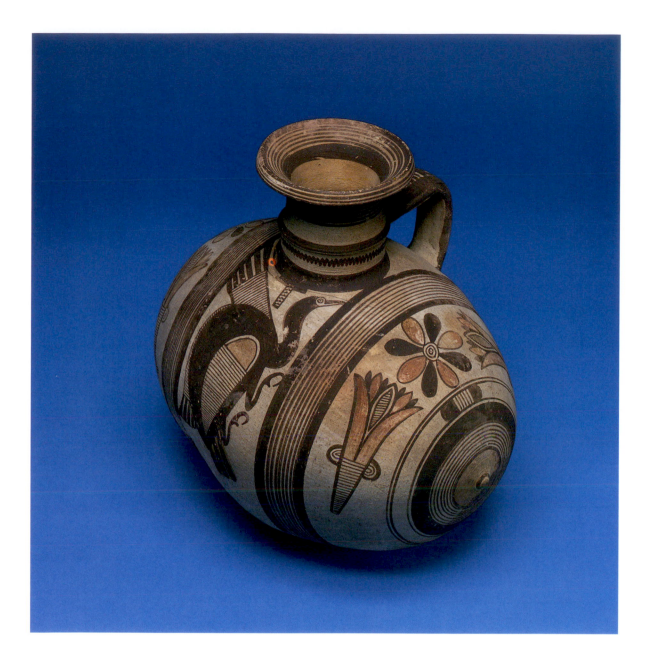

115. *Bichrome Flask*

Cyprus; Cypriot Iron Age, 11th century BC
Terracotta; W. 31 cm (12.2 in.)
MS5711

This sturdy and capacious vessel, designed for carrying liquids, is
decorated with a bird at its center and twin lotuses and a rosette in
each lateral zone.

116. *Tarentine Red-figure Bull's Head Rhyton*

Taranto, Italy; ca. 350–320 BC
Terracotta; L. 24 cm (9.5 in.)
L-64-227 (on loan, Philadelphia Museum of Art)

Because of its shape, this rhyton, a type of drinking vessel, cannot be
set down until it has been drained of its contents. Taras (later
Tarentum) was an important Greek settlement in south Italy.

117. *Etruscan/Faliscan Commander's Crested Helmet*

Narce, Tomb 43, Italy; end of 8th century BC
Bronze; H. 43 cm (16.9 in.)
MS850

Boldly decorated with geometric patterns, the sheer size of this battle accoutrement allowed its wearer to be identified at a distance by his followers. This is one of two helmets found buried with the same warrior.

118. *Portrait of a Roman Matron*

Probably from Sardinia, Italy; ca. AD 10–20
Marble; H. 36 cm (14.2 in.)
MS4919

The Roman ideal of the modest woman with strength of character is expressed clearly in this powerful, individualized portrait. The close dating of the sculpture comes from a comparison of the hairstyle with that of portraits of Livia and Julia, the wife and daughter of Augustus.

119. *Wheelmade Mycenaean Kylix*

Mainland Greece; Late Helladic IIIA:2 (ca. 1300 BC)
Terracotta; H. 21 cm (8.3 in)
MS5701

Kylikes are the drinking cups par excellence for the wealthy, turning up
in large numbers in all Mycenaean settlements. Although most are
plain, this piece is decorated with a facing octopus rendered in a
stylized fashion typical of this period in Mycenaean art.

120. *Basket Earrings with Sheet-metal Pendants*

Troad region, Turkey; mid-3rd millennium BC
Gold; L. 12.7 (5 in.), 12 cm (4.7 in.)
66-6-11A,B

These are part of the Museum's collection of jewelry reportedly
recovered near Troy. Each basket is fashioned from looped wires
soldered together. Plates made up of rings are suspended from the baskets to which are attached seven loop-in-loop chains.

121. *Selection of Greek Coins*

Left: Silver decadrachm with a racing four-horse chariot and water nymph with dolphins; signed by Euaenetos, a renowned coin designer. Minted by Syracuse (Sicily), Italy; ca. 400–375 BC. Dia. 3.4 cm (1.3 in.) 29-126-41

Center: Silver tetradrachm with Athena and her favorite bird, the owl, which holds an olive branch, symbolizing Athen's lucrative export, olive oil. Minted by Athens, Greece; 449–410 BC. Dia. 2.4 cm (0.93 in.) 29-126-404

Right: Gold octodrachm depicting Queen Arsinöe II and a double cornucopia. The redoubtable Arsinöe was the sister and wife of Ptolemy. Minted in Alexandria, Egypt; 169–145 BC. Dia. 3.0 cm (1.2 in.) 29-126-546

122. *Corinthian Lidded Pyxis*

By the Geladakis Painter; ca. 595–570 BC
Terracotta; Dia. 16.5 cm (6.5 in.)
MS5482. Photographs by Maria Daniels for the Perseus Project

This type of vessel was perhaps originally made of wood or woven rushes and was used to hold either women's cosmetics or jewelry. On this terracotta pyxis, the decoration consists of orientalizing sirens, griffins, and panthers. Corinth exported its pottery around the Mediterranean.

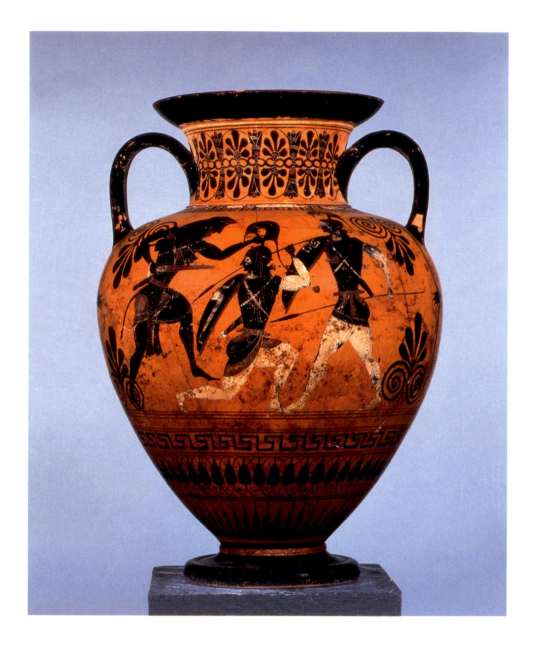

123. *Attic Black-figure Amphora*

In the manner of the Lysippides Painter; ca. 530–525 BC
Terracotta; H. 41 cm (16.1 in.)
MS5467. Photograph by Maria Daniels for the Perseus Project

Heracles fights with two Amazons, a race of female warriors thought to live on the fringes of the civilized world. Mythological combat scenes embody the Greeks' preoccupation with struggle, as well as their love for detailed battle narratives, and are a hallmark of Archaic Greek art.

Mesopotamia

124. Tablets with Economic Texts

Top: Probably from Lagash; ca. 2500 BC
Limestone; W. 12.8 cm (5 in.)
Bottom: Nippur; ca. 2400–2200 BC
Clay; W. 6.5 cm (2.6 in.)
CBS10,000, N283

Top: This stone tablet records plots of land and the prices paid for each, including payments in copper, barley, and pigs. Early forms of the cuneiform signs are aesthetically pleasing, but difficult to understand.
Bottom: An account in Sumerian of an official's income from various sources over a three-year period. Such economic documents allow a detailed look at the economy and society of early Mesopotamia.

125. *The Babylonian Flood Story*

Nippur, Iraq; ca. 1800 BC
Clay; W. 13 cm (5 in.)
B10673 + B10562

Many tablets from ancient Mesopotamia preserve accounts of the
Flood, very similar to the one described in Genesis. This is the only
known version written in the Sumerian language. The hero of this
account is named not Noah but Ziusudra, "Life of distant days."

126. Terracotta "Squeeze," Front and Back

Nippur; Neo-Babylonian period (626–539 BC)
W. 6 cm (2.4 in.), H. 3.8 cm (1.5 in.)
CBS16106

A lively interest in the past was encouraged by kings of the Neo-Babylonian period, as they attempted to unify a long-divided land. King Nabonidus took an impression, or squeeze (top), from a stone original of the king Shar-kali-sharri, who lived over 1500 years before him; Nabonidus then wrote his own account of finding it on the back.

127. *Brick Stamp*

Nippur; ca. 2200 BC
Clay; W. 14 cm (5.5 in.), handle broken off
L-29-309

The inscription—"Shar-kali-sharri, king of Akkade, builder of Enlil's temple"—is written backwards because it was used by construction workers to stamp large bricks for the foundations of the temple of the chief god, Enlil.

128. *Documents in Clay*

Top: Murashu archive; 5th century BC. Bottom: Nippur; Old Babylonian Period (ca. 1800 BC)
W. (top) 7.5 cm (3 in.); W. (bottom tablet) 4.6 cm (1.8 in.)
CBS5304, CBS4711

Top: Contracts such as this one for the supply of dates were still written in Akkadian. The tablet's owner would have been unable to read it, so a summary in Aramaic was added.
Bottom: An Akkadian letter from a man named Ibi-ilum to Shu-ili, with its envelope (left). Envelopes protected the original from tampering.

129. *Votive Figurine*

Nintu temple, Khafaje (ancient Tutub), Iraq
Early Dynastic II (2650–2550 BC)
Gypsum; H. 23 cm (9 in.)
37-15-28

Statuettes such as this male figure, common in Early
Dynastic Mesopotamia (2900–2350 BC), were votives, gifts
dedicated to deities for the well-being and life of their
donors. This is one of the finest examples recovered from
sites in the lower Diyala River basin, northeast of modern
Baghdad. It shows more realistic proportions and naturalis-
tic details, such as the double chin and slight smile, than
many other contemporary statuettes found in the Diyala
excavations.

130. *Sarcophagus Lid*

Beth Shean (ancient Scythopolis), Israel; Iron Age IA (1200–1000 BC)
Baked clay; H. 60.3 cm (23.5 in.)
29-103-789

Archaeologists characterize such coffin lids as "natural" or "grotesque," depending on their degree of realism. This lid is in the "natural" style. The coffins reflect Egyptian practices and date to the last phase of Egypt's empire in ancient Canann, ca. 1250–1150 BC.

131. *Female Figurine*

Tureng Tepe, Iran; Tureng Tepe IIIB Period (ca. 3500–2900 BC)
Ceramic; H. 18.3 cm (7 in.)
32-41-25

Although not clothed, this woman is adorned with many bracelets, necklaces, and an elaborate headdress. The figurine was a burial offering.

132. *Electrum Fluted Tumbler*

Royal Cemetery, Ur, Iraq; Early Dynastic III (2550–2450 BC)
H. 15.2 cm (ca. 6 in.)
B17691

This graceful fluted tumbler, from the tomb of Puabi, Ur's queen, has chased herringbone bands at top and bottom next to which are double zigzags. A rosette with eight petals decorates the base, and a loop for the attachment of a wire or strong handle was hammered out of the rim.

133. *Puabi's Headdress*

Royal Cemetery, Ur, Iraq; Early Dynastic III (2550–2450 BC)
Gold, lapis lazuli, carnelian, shell; W. of comb 11 cm (4.29 in.)
B16692a,b, B16693, B17709–12, 98-9-9a,b

Puabi's headdress included a frontlet with beads and pendant gold rings, two wreaths with poplar leaves, a wreath with willow leaves and inlaid rosettes, and a string of lapis lazuli beads. The comb would have been inserted in her hair at the back, leaving the flowers floating over her head.

134. *"Ram Caught in a Thicket"*

"Great Death Pit," Ur, Iraq; Early Dynastic III (2550–2450 BC)
Gold, silver, lapis lazuli, copper, shell, red limestone, bitumen; H. 42.6 cm (16.6 in.)
30-12-702

The "Ram Caught in a Thicket" was so named because it closely matches
the imagery of Genesis 22:13. The statuette would have supported a
tray. The many materials used create a colorful effect typical of early
Mesopotamian composite art.

135. Lyre with Bearded Bull's Head and Inlaid Panel

Royal Cemetery, Ur, Iraq; Early Dynastic III (2550–2450 BC)
Wood, lapis lazuli, gold, silver, shell, bitumen; H. (head): 35.6 cm (13.9 in.)
B17694

The lyre's panel depicts a heroic figure grasping human-headed bulls above and animals acting as humans below. In the third panel, for example, an animal orchestra includes an ass playing a bull-headed lyre similar to the one the inlay decorates.

136. Cylinder Seals and Modern Impressions

Royal Cemetery, Ur, Iraq; Early Dynastic III (2550–2450 BC)
Lapis lazuli; H. (top) 4 cm, (bottom) 4.1 cm (1.6 in.)
B16728, B16852

Cylinder seals are unique to ancient Near Eastern civilizations. They were markers of identity, important in administrative and legal actions. The upper seal, found with Puabi the queen, depicts banquet scenes featuring women, the lower depicts heroes protecting animals from feline predators.

137. *Vessel in the Shape of an Ostrich Egg*

Royal Cemetery, Ur, Iraq; Early Dynastic III (2550–2450 BC)
Gold, lapis lazuli, red limestone, shell, bitumen; H. 14.6 cm (5.7 in.)
B16692

This vessel is made from a single sheet of gold hammered from the inside. The top and bottom of the egg are decorated with geometric mosaics of lapis lazuli, red limestone, and shell set into bitumen, a tar-like substance.

138. *Inlaid Silver Cosmetic Box Lid*

Royal Cemetery, Ur, Iraq; Early Dynastic III (2550–2450 BC)
Silver, shell, and lapis lazuli; Dia. across lid 6.4 cm (2.5 in.)
B16744A

This is probably one of two semicircular sections that formed the lid of a segmented container. The lid is carved from a single piece of shell. A second piece of shell carved in relief and depicting a lion attacking a sheep or goat is set into the center of the lid.

139. Gold Chain

Beth Shean (ancient Scythopolis), Israel; late 6th–early 7th century AD
L. 77 cm (30 in.)
31-50-212

The chain has a central medallion with a filigree pattern and links in the form of stylized flowers. It was found beneath the floor in a small room off the chapel of a Byzantine monastery. It was likely buried at the time of the Arab invasion.

140. Inlaid Goat's Head

Iraq; Early Dynastic III (2550–2250 BC)
Copper alloy, shell, red stone; H. 22 cm (8.6 in.)
29-20-3

The range of the markhor goat, known for its spiraling horns, has historically covered Turkmenistan, Uzbekistan, Tajikstan, Afghanistan, Pakistan, and northern India. This piece, created by lost-wax casting, is one of two goat heads acquired during the 1899–1900 campaign at Nippur.

141. Painted Islamic Tiles

Iran; 18th century AD
Ceramic; W. (bottom l.) 16.5 cm (6.4 in.), (others) 18.5 cm (7.2 in.)
2001-15-47, 2001-15-48, 2001-15-49

These white glazed tiles have underglazes of green, yellow, black, cobalt
blue, pink, and red. In the center of each tile is a portrait; the two
ladies and the man (top tile) wear colorful garments and headdresses.

142. *Loculus Cover with Portrait of an Elite Woman*

Tadmor (ancient Palmyra); 3rd century AD
Limestone; H. 50 cm (19.5 in.)
CBS 8904

Loculi sealed burial niches in large subterranean tombs or aboveground funerary towers. The woman's pose, with the left hand adjusting her veil, as well as details of her jewelry and clothing date the portrait to the 3rd century, when Palmyra was at its height.

143. *Illustration from Nizami's* Khamsa

Shiraz, Iran; AD 1584
Parchment, ink; H. 37.4 cm (14.6 in.)
NEP-33

The poet Nizami was born around AD 1140 in what is today Azerbaijan.
This miniature is from his *Khamsa* (quintet), an epic poem of five stories,
and illustrates one of King Bahram's adventures in slaying a dragon. The
Khamsa is the most beloved storybook in Persian culture.

152. *Mortuary Mask* (Tatanua)

Northern New Ireland, Papua New Guinea
Late 19th–early 20th century
Wood, vegetable fiber, cotton, feathers, snail opercula, pigment;
H. 38 cm (15.5 in.)
P4555

Tatanua are worn by male dancers in large-scale, multi-village mortuary celebrations. Preparation for performances with these powerful masks involves weeks of ritual avoidance of any kind of contact with women.

153. *Carved and Painted Head*

Melville Island, Northern Territory, Australia; collected 1954
Wood, pigment; H. 46 cm (18.1 in.)
55-17-11

When it was collected on Melville Island in the 1950s, this carved and painted head was an example of a new form of art. The painting reproduces designs of face decoration used during traditional Tiwi funeral ceremonies.

154. *Ceremonial Axe*

New Caledonia; 19th century
Greenstone, wood, cloth, coconut shell and fiber, fur, shells; H. 55 cm (21.5 in.)
P2126

In New Caledonia, ceremonial axes were symbols of power and prestige. They were brandished by orators and carried as batons by important men. As valuables, they also figured in chiefly gifts and exchanges.

155. *Pendant* (Hei Tiki)

New Zealand; collected in 1777
Greenstone (nephrite); H. 8.3 cm (3.2 in.)
P2317

Greenstone pendants were, and are, treasured Maori ornaments. Their value derives from the hours of labor required to carve the hard material and from association with the ancestors through whose hands the carvings have passed from generation to generation.

156. *Pubic Ornament*

Kimberley Region, Western Australia; collected before 1911
Pearl shell, red ochre, human hair; H. 17 cm (6.6 in.)
P3091A

Engraved pearl shell disks, made by Aborigines on the northwest coast of Australia, were highly valued objects of exchange, traded hundreds of miles into the interior. They were used in rain-making rituals and worn as ornaments.

157. *Dress Shield* (Kalasag)

Mindanao, Philippines; collected 1905–1910
Wood, hair, rattan peel; H. (including hair) 102 cm (39.8 in.)
P2977B

Such dress shields were carried by Bagobo men of southern Mindanao at festivals and ceremonies. In fighting, the Bagobo used shields of this type for fending off knives and intercepting spears and arrows.

158. *Carving of Rhinoceros Hornbill* (Kenyalang)

Sarawak, Borneo; collected 1898
Wood, pigment; L. 77.5 cm (30.2 in.)
P815A

A rhinoceros hornbill carving is the centerpiece of a religious ceremony celebrated by the Ibanic peoples of Borneo. In the course of the ceremony, the carving is ritually transformed into a spiritual messenger to a major deity, Singalong Burong.

159. *Food Dish*

Wuvulu (Maty) Island, Papua New Guinea; late 19th–early 20th century
Wood; L. 47 cm (18.3 in.)
P3482B

The culture of Wuvulu Island, located in the Bismarck Archipelago, is
Micronesian rather than Melanesian. Skilled woodworkers, the people
of Wuvulu used shell cutting tools to produce elegantly simple food
bowls like this one.

160. *Suspension Hook*

Yamanum Village, middle Sepik River, Papua New Guinea; collected 1913
Wood, pigment; H. 104.5 cm (40.8 in.)
29-50-342

In the area of the middle Sepik, suspension hooks are found in both family dwellings and cult houses. They are used for hanging food in net bags to foil rats and for making offerings of chicken and betel nut to guardian spirits.

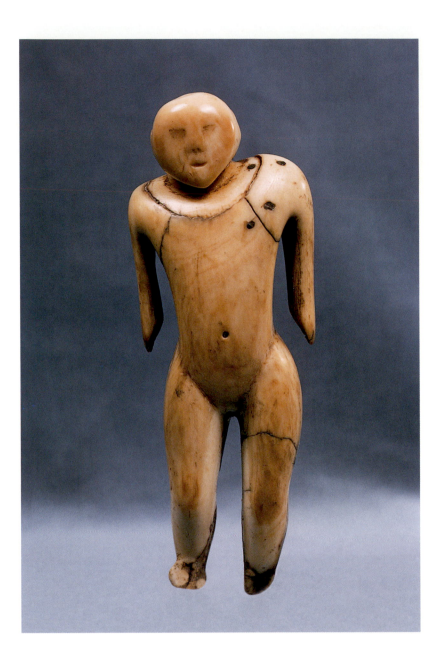

161. *Carved Ivory Figure*

Fiji; collected mid- to late 19th century
Sperm whale tooth; H. 20 cm (7.8 in.)
18194A

This is one of a handful of small whale ivory figures collected in Fiji during the second half of the 19th century. Little is known about their function and significance. They seem to have been objects of reverence, but not worship.

162. *Shadow Puppet*

Java; late 19th–early 20th century
Hide, bamboo, pigments; H. (figure) 29.5 cm (11.5 in.)
29-91-20

This shadow puppet represents Narayana, an incarnation of Kresna (Krishna). In an important cycle of Javanese plays based on the Indian epic Mahabarata, Kresna is a powerful ally of the five Pandawa brothers in their struggle against their cousins, the Korawa.

163. *Ceremonial Cloth* (Pua) *(detail)*

Borneo; collected 1896–1898
Cotton; L. 2.47 m (ca. 8 ft.)
P603A

Such ceremonial cloths, woven by women of the Ibanic peoples of Borneo, are imbued with supernatural power. Once used to receive trophy heads into the longhouse, they are now hung to mark off sacred space for the performance of rituals.

164. *Canoe Bow Piece*

Near Wellington, North Island, New Zealand; collected in the 1870s
Wood, abalone shell; L. 99.5 cm (38.8 in.)
18128

This carved bow piece for a Maori war canoe is of the style called *piitau*, which features two large pierced scrolls and, at the very front, a defiant human figure with tongue protruding and arms thrown back.

165. *Sago Bowl* (Kamana)

Timbunke Village, middle Sepik River, Papua New Guinea; collected 1913
Clay, pigment; H. 18.5 cm (7.2 in.)
29-50-350

Bowls for eating sago, a starch derived from sago palms, are produced in
the Sawos area for sale and trade to villages along the middle Sepik.
Although beautifully decorated, they are not ceremonial vessels. When
in use, they rest on cane rings around the cooking pot.

166. *Carrying Bag* (Kabir)

Mindanao, Philippine Islands; collected 1905–1910
Hemp, glass beads, brass bells; H. (without straps) 47.5 cm (18.5 in.)
P5007

Bags are used by Bagobo men of southern Mindanao for carrying personal effects on their backs. Like the jackets and trousers worn by the Bagobo, they are made of hemp and ornamented with glass beads. Brass bells jingle as the wearer walks.

167A. *Fighting Jacket (front)*

Sarawak, Borneo; collected 1896–1898
Sun bear skin, rhinoceros hornbill feathers and beaks, shell, glass beads;
L. (without feathers) 83 cm (32.4 in.)
P1152

167B. Fighting Jacket (back)

In 19th century Borneo, fighting was an essential part of life. Fighting ability and bravery were much admired, and fighting gear was made of rare and spectacular materials. This fighting jacket was worn by Madang men.

168. *Ritual Communion Bowl* (Apira Ni Mwane)

Santa Catalina, Eastern Solomon Islands, late 19th–early 20th century
Wood, shell, pigment, vegetable fiber; L. 67 cm (ca. 26 in.)
67-5-1

Ordinary food bowls are undecorated, but bowls used in periodic ritual meals, in which each member of the congregation communes with his own patron deity, are elaborately carved and inlaid with shell.

169. *Coconut Grater Stool* (Duai)

Made by Soses Tara, Nukuoro, Caroline Islands; collected 1964
Wood, shell, coconut fiber; L. 56 cm (21.8 in.)
65-8-1

A Micronesian coconut grater is a stool with a projection at the front
to which something sharp has been lashed. This stool has a serrated
piece of shell across which the open side of a split coconut is rubbed.

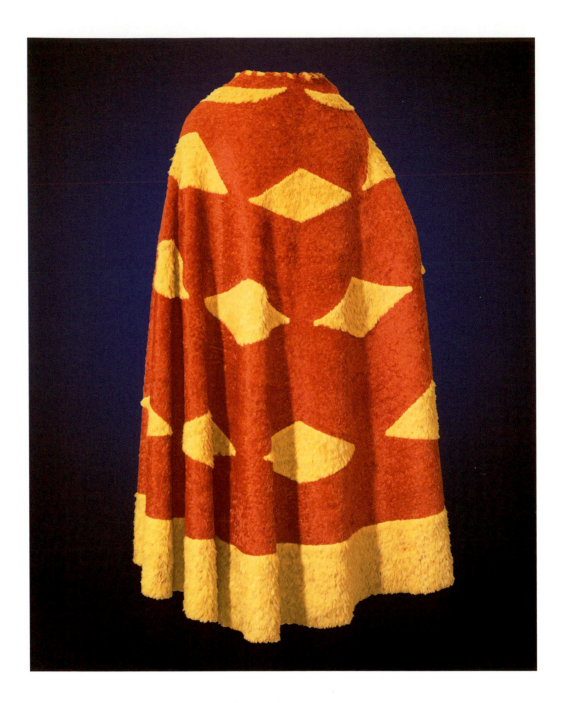

170. *Feather Cloak* ('Ahu 'Ula)

Hawaiian Islands; 19th century
Olonaa fiber, feathers; L. 1.38 m (4.5 ft.)
29-58-155

Feather cloaks were an essential part of aristocratic regalia in ancient
Hawaii. They were made and worn only by men. The feathers are red—
the color of the aristocrats and gods—and rare, highly prized yellow.

171. *Featherwork Gorget* (Taumi)

Society Islands; 18th century
Coconut fiber, twigs, feathers, shark teeth, dog hair; W. across top without hair
ca. 57 cm (22 in.)
29-58-11

These showy breast ornaments, worn by warriors in ancient Tahiti, were presented to important 18th century visitors such as James Cook and William Bligh and were traded to sailors for red feathers.

172. *Bark Cloth* (Masi) *(detail)*

Fiji; collected in the 1870s
Felted bark, pigment; L. 4.87 m (ca. 15.8 ft.)
18182A

This bark cloth is of a style typical of a particular region in northern
Fiji, the Cakaudrove area. The large geometric design elements are
hand painted; the star shapes and narrow bands of fine brown patterns
enclosing them are stenciled.

173. *Lime Container*

Kambringi Village, middle Sepik River, Papua New Guinea; collected 1913
Bamboo, wood, rattan peel, pigment; H. 77 cm (30 in.)
29-50-557A

From South Asia to the islands of Melanesia, people chew betel, a quid consisting of areca palm nuts, betel pepper leaves, and slaked lime. The plug of this lime container, which would be at the bottom when in use, is decorated with a carved bird on a crocodile head.

European Archaeology

174. Flint Core and Handaxes (Bifaces)

Top: Levallois core, Grand-Pressigny area of southwest France;
Middle Paleolithic (250,000–40,000 BC)
Bottom left: handaxe, Stoke Newington, London, England; Lower
Paleolithic (ca. 300,000 BC)
Bottom right: handaxe, Somme, Amiens, Saint-Acheul, France
H. of core 11.3 cm (4.4 in.)
12942A, EU2428, L-37-966

Neandertal flintknappers throughout Europe, the Near East,
and Africa would prepare a core in such a way that they
could produce a single flake (removed from this piece) of a
specified size and shape.

    Bifaces are the characteristic tool of the Lower
Paleolithic. Early hominids of Eurasia and Africa would
shape these pieces by removing many small flakes from the
edges. They were probably used as all-purpose tools for
butchering game.

Physical Anthropology

179. The Morton Collection

Top row: 427, 663, 547
Center row: 429, 1190, 606
Bottom row: 926, 1249, 1307

The Morton Collection contains about 1500 skulls collected in the early to mid-19th century. There are representative specimens from virtually all populations on the planet, making it a unique resource for study. For example, the chips and lines in the teeth of an individual skull can tell us about his or her health and diet. Put together with an analysis of the chemicals composing the bones, we can contribute to knowledge about the source of nutrients in the diet. Then adding information obtained from other skulls, we get a study record of an entire population.

180. *"A Burmese Villager"*

By Philip A. Klier (ca. 1845–1911)
Ca. 1880
Albumen print; H. 26.7 cm (10.5 in.)
T4-2518

Many of the images in the Museum Archives' extensive collection of 19th century photography are colored by the attitudes and mores of Western society of the time. It is in this vein that commercial photographer Philip A. Klier, like many other photographers of his time, depicted a society at the end of the 19th century—in this case Burma—that both helped create, and conformed to, Western ideas of the "exotic."

A BURMESE VILLAGER. 500.
P. KLIER. RANGOON.

181. *"Caffée Arabe"*

By Zangaki (active 1870s–1890s); ca. 1880, probably Cairo, Egypt
Albumen print, mounted; H. 28 cm (11 in.)
T4-2495

Little is known about C. and G. Zangaki, who ran a successful commercial photography studio in Egypt in the late 19th century. Their images catered to European and American tourists and the romantic attitudes toward the Middle East and the Holy Lands of the time.

182. *"Rural Tunisian Dancers"*

By Rudolf Lehnert (1878–1948) and Ernst Landrock (1880–1957); 1910, Tunis
Photogravure; H. 24.3 cm (9.6 in.)
T4-2496

Lehnert and Landrock took photographs in North Africa, Egypt, and
Palestine from 1904 to 1930. Their work conveys their view of the atmos-
phere and life of the Orient, with picturesque street scenes, mysterious
Bedouins, quiet oases, and desert idylls.

183. *"Cafard" (Gremlins)*

By Alfred Bendiner (1899–1964); 1960, Tikal, Guatemala
Pen and ink drawing on paper; H. 37 cm (14.6 in.)
S8-146980

Architect Alfred Bendiner is best known for his caricatures, which although humorous show a deep understanding of people and life. He worked on two archaeological projects for the University of Pennsylvania Museum and produced a number of drawings while in the field.

184. *Lintel III from Temple IV, Tikal, Guatemala*

By Annie Hunter (?–1928); ca. 1895
Pencil drawing on board; H. 32.2 cm (12.7 in.)
T4-2501

British artist Annie G. Hunter achieved renown working for Alfred P. Maudslay, pioneer archaeologist of the ancient Maya. The accuracy and detail of her renderings of Maya inscriptions and iconography are unparalleled.

185. *"Patagonian Woman (Lorenza) with Her Dog Kak"*

By Jessie Tarbox Beals (1870–1942); 1904, St. Louis World's Fair
Gelatin silver print; H. 24 cm (9.5 in.)
T4-2497

Beals, the first woman newspaper photographer in the United States, was official photographer for the 1904 St. Louis World's Fair. She recorded many of the anthropological "exhibits," indigenous people who were brought from exotic locations for public education and entertainment.

186. *"A Son of the Desert—Navaho"*

By Edward S. Curtis (1868–1952); 1904
Platinum print, mounted; H. 40.5 cm (15.95 in.)
T2-2367

Curtis is known for his beautiful, though often staged, portraits of American Indians. In *The North American Indian*, produced over a period of thirty years, he assembled over twenty volumes of plates depicting native tribes of the U.S. and Canada.

187. *Japanese Women*

Photographer unknown, possibly Felice Beato (1825–ca. 1908), Raimund von
Stillfried (1839–1911), or Kusakabe Kimbei (1841–1934); 1890
Albumen print, tinted, mounted; H. 24 cm (9.5 in.)
T4-2499

Beato opened a studio in Japan in 1862–1863, producing hand-colored
views of Japanese life and people. His studio was purchased by Baron von
Stillfried in 1877, who in turn sold his photographic stock to Kimbei.

188. *"Women Playing Ball" (detail)*

By Carl Matches (ca. 1856–1914); 1877
Pencil drawing on ledger page; H. 17 cm (6.7 in.)
T4-2539

Carl Matches (Chi-I-Se-Duh) was a Southern Cheyenne warrior arrested in 1875 and taken to Fort Marion, Florida. While there, he made drawings of his life before captivity as well as scenes of Fort Marion, employing the pictographic tradition of the Plains Indians.

189. *"Wind River Peak"*

By William Henry Jackson (1843–1942); ca. 1870, Wyoming
Albumen print, mounted; H. 24.5 cm (9.7 in.)
T4-2500

Jackson was the leading photographer of the American West in the
19th century. In 1870 he joined the U.S. Geological and Geographical
Survey, and his photographs of Yellowstone helped turn it into the first
national park. His later work documented the conquest of the frontier.

190. *"Village and Pyramids during the Flooding of the Nile"*
By Maison Bonfils; ca. 1890
Albumen print, mounted; H. 22 cm (8.7 in.)
T2-941

Maison Bonfils, located in Beirut, Lebanon, was one of the best-known
and most prolific commercial photographic studios of the last decades of
the Ottoman Empire. The family of Félix Bonfils photographed people,
townscapes, and ancient ruins before a time of radical social change.

191. "Ancient Costume of the Kandyans, Ceylon"

By Charles T. Scowen (active 1873–1893); ca. 1870
Albumen print; H. 21.3 cm (8.4 in.)
T4-2494

Scowen and Co. was one of the most accomplished and successful photographic firms working in Sri Lanka (former Ceylon). Their images, produced for the tourist market as well as for commerce and industry, included local views, ethnic portraiture, and indigenous customs.

Index

Concordance

Plate	Object No.	Neg. No.
1	72-33-1	T4-2507
2	29-12-188	T4-526
3	70-18-1	T4-6
4	AF5154	T35-1387
5	AF5120	T35-1428
6	30-10-1	T4-9
7	62-3-1	T4-2502
8	79-18-1	T35-1355
9	29-59-11	T35-1415
10	87-13-109	T4-2508
11	AF5360	T4-2503
12	AF5108	T4-4
13	29-94-10	T4-627
14	68-18-1	T35-1417
15	29-12-68	T4-827
16	AF2048	T4-2504
16	AF5085	T4-2504
17	29-93-5	T35-1365
18	AF35	T35-1426
19	29-59-207	T35-1382
19	29-59-181	T35-1382
19	29-59-169	T35-1382
20	82-1-1	T4-523
21	77-4-1	T35-1403
22	29-12-227	T4-490
23	29-12-92	T35-1349
24	NA4972	T4-2431
25	29-77-422	T4-343
26	29-47-184	T4-826
27	38870	T4-2947
28	L-84-2124	T4-2603
28	L-84-2123	T4-2603
29	2002-9-2	T4-2607
30	NA5389	T4-3060
31	L-84-1391A,B	T4-2606
32	NA8502	T4-205
33	NA7890	T4-2648
34	76-23-1	T4-471
35	69-24-1	T4-2958
36	68-32-2b	T4-2965
37	38-14-1	T4-112
37	painting	T4-2618
38	40-13-198	T4-662
38	40-13-33	T4-641
38	40-13-28	T4-643
39	40-13-2	T4-541
40	61-1-1	T4-3043
41	NA5897	T4-2985
41	NA5900	T4-2985
42	NA5194	T4-3005
43	84-27-1	T4-2948
44	SA2751	T4-320
45	SA4604	T35-3384
46	43531	T4-2605
47	CG852611-6459	T35-3385
48	SA2702	T4-300
49	SA4611	T4-2564
50	CG2003-2-1	T4-2946
51	39-20-70	T35-608
52	SA1077	T4-2563
52	SA4559	T4-2563
52	SA4560	T4-2563
52	SA4699	T4-2563
53	SA2490	T4-2565
54	31017	T4-2604
55	C408	T4-2569
56	C681A,B	T4-2647
57	C395	T4-171
58	52-23-71	T4-73
59	C68A,B	T4-2633, T4-2634
60	C404	T4-2568
61	54-6-6	T4-2570
62	C405	T4-417
63	C466	T4-219
64	C400	35mm by N. Steinhardt
65	44-16-1A,B	T4-2639
66	C66A,B	T4-173
67	29-96-339	T4-2628
67	29-96-338	T4-2628
68	29-96-346	T4-2625
69	85-28-5	T4-2635
70	29-69-2	Philadelphia Museum of Art
71	29-68-1	T4-797
72	77-5-5	T35-2027
73	43-12-2	T4-2632
74	29-64-232	T4-2637
75	53-14-1	T4-2631
76	60-5-4	T4-2636
77	29-88-2	T4-2638
78	E10980	T4-1107
79	E13643	T4-2025
80	53-20-1a	T4-1171
81	29-70-19	T4-1198
82	E12615a	T4-1159
83	E2148	T4-1172
84	E16214	T4-2512
84	E16315	T4-2512
85	40-19-3	T4-1114
86	E10751	T4-1102
87	E14295	T4-1095
88	E635	35mm by D. Silverman
89	E14368 a,b	T4-1139
90	57-18-1	T4-1080
91	E16012	T4-1176, T4-1177
92	E2775	T4-1161
93	31-27-303	T4-1166
94	E9191	T4-1126
94	E9195	T4-1126
95	E9217	T4-1106
96	E14344b,c	T4-1168, T4-1169
97	E14350	T4-1087
98	E7519	T4-1183
99	E7794	T4-1184
99	E7922	T4-1184
99	E7925	T4-1184
100	E8157	T4-547
101	MS5462	T4-604
102	MS4021	T4-2714
103	MS5005	T4-2527
104	MS4017	T4-2734

Plate	Object No.	Neg. No.
105	69-14-1	T4-607
106	MS1801	T4-2679
107	34-1-1	MS 35mm
108	30-33-2A	MS 35mm
108	30-33-1	MS 35mm
109	MS5134	Digital image courtesy of S. Fleming
110	MS3459	T4-2725
111	L-64-185	T4-603
112	29-128-904	MS 35mm
112	29-128-900	MS 35mm
112	29-128 -879	MS 35mm
112	29-128-552	MS 35mm
112	29-128-63A	MS 35mm
113	MS4028	T4-2521
114	MS2730	T4-2522
115	MS5711	T4-2523
116	L-64-227	T4-2519
117	MS850	T4-2877
118	MS4919	T4-2865
119	MS5701	T4-2520
120	66-6-11a,b	T4-2343
121	29-126-41	T4-602 (obv.); MS 35mm (rev.)
121	29-126-404	MS 35mms
121	29-126-546	T4-2743 (obv.); MS 35mm (rev.)
122	MS5482	PP 1991.07.1232 (whole vessel)
		PP 1991.07.1235 (dtl.)
123	MS5467	PP 1991-07-0997
124	CBS10,000	T4-2615
124	N283	T4-2615
125	B10673 + B10562	T4-2332 (rev.)
126	CBS16106	T4-2612, T4-2613
128	CBS4711	T4-2614
128	CBS5304	T4-2614
127	L-29-309	T4-2611
129	37-15-28	T4-2346
130	29-103-789	T4-65
131	32-41-25	T4-31
132	B17691	T4-2180
133	B16692	T4-2100
133	B16693	T4-2100
133	B17709–12	T4-2100
134	30-12-702	T4-2054
135	B17694	T4-888, T4-480
136	B16852	T4-2090, T4-2091
136	B16728	T4-2074, T4-2075
137	B16692	T4-2071
138	B16744A	T4-2067
139	31-50-212	T4-2516, T4-2517 (dtl.)
140	29-20-3	T4-2758
141	2001-15-49	T4-2515
141	2001-15-48	T4-2515
141	2001-15-47	T4-2515
142	CBS8904	T4-2795
143	NEP-33	T35-2047
144	B16664	T4-2768
145	29-21-1	T4-2774
146	NEP-17	T4-2562
147	33-22-177	T4-2627
148	37-15-95	T4-2561
148	38-10-96	T4-2561
148	38-10-95	T4-2561
148	38-10-92	T4-2561
148	37-15-81	T4-2561
148	37-15-80	T4-2561
148	32-20-158	T4-2773
149	NEP-12	T4-2513, T4-2514 (dtl.)

Plate	Object No.	Neg. No.
150	29-93-46	T4-2629
151	61-3-3	T4-174
152	P4555	T4-2609
153	55-17-11	T4-2594
154	P2126	T4-2593
155	P2317	T4-497
156	P3091A	T4-2596
157	P2977B	T4-538
158	P815A	T4-273
159	P3482B	T4-2597
160	29-50-342	T4-2600
161	18194A	T35-1243
162	29-91-20	T4-2602
163	P603A	T4-124
164	18128	T4-2601
165	29-50-350	T35-1222
166	P5007	T4-2592
167	P1152	T4-115, T4-116
168	67-5-1	T4-2595
169	65-8-1	T4-2591
170	29-58-155	T4-1069, T4-1070
171	29-58-11	T4-182
172	18182A	OC-TM-R4:18
173	29-50-557A	T4-2598
174	L-37-966	T4-2653
174	EU2428	T4-2653
174	12942A	T4-2653
175	EU1557	T4-2652
175	EU1576	T4-2652
175	EU2333A–C	T4-2652
175	EU2615	T4-2652
175	62-13-6	T4-2652
176	65-25-255	T4-2650
176	29-218-1	T4-2650
176	65-25-70	T4-2650
176	65-25-69	T4-2650
176	65-25-63	T4-2650
176	65-25-28	T4-2650
177	65-25-254B	T4-2651
177	65-25-164A,C	T4-2651
177	65-25-100	T4-2651
177	65-25-92A	T4-2651
177	65-25-73	T4-2651
177	65-25-68	T4-2651
178	42-30-122	T4-2654
178	70-4-1	T4-2654
179	427	T4-2526
179	429	T4-2524
179	547	T4-2526
179	606	T4-2524
179	663	T4-2526
179	926	T4-2525
179	1190	T4-2524
179	1249	T4-2525
179	1307	T4-2525
180		T4-2518
181		T4-2495
182		T4-2496
183		S8-146980
184		T4-2501
185		T4-2497
186		T2-2367
187		T4-2499
189		T4-2500
190		T2-941
191		T4-2494

MS = Mediterranean Section; PP = Perseus Project

On a Final Note

Putting together this book involved the cooperation and goodwill of a great many people throughout the Museum; I am grateful to them all. From the outset, I was guided by the committee assembled to oversee the book's production: Dr. Gerald Margolis, Dr. Walda Metcalf, Dr. Harold Dibble, Gillian Wakely, Susan West, Kevin Lamp, and Suzanne Sheehan Becker. My thanks especially to Kevin for taking on the intricacies of coordinating gallery photography.

First and foremost, this project would not have succeeded without the hard work of the section keepers—Adria Katz, Dwaune Latimer, Lynn Makowsky, Janet Monge, Micah Toomey, Jennifer Wegner, Shannon White, Bill Wierzbowski, and Lucy Fowler Williams—and the curators and research staff—Drs. Ann Brownlee, Keith DeVries, Harold Dibble, Clark Erickson, Gregory Possehl, Robert Preucel, Irene Romano, Robert Sharer, David Silverman, Steve Tinney, Josef Wegner, Donald White, and Richard Zettler. Of equal importance were the creative efforts of Francine Sarin and Jennifer Chiappardi in the Photo Studio; they gave me gentle and invaluable instruction in the possibilities and difficulties of object photography. Archivist Alex Pezzati and Photographic Archivist Charles S. Kline provided much-appreciated assistance in identifying and gathering images for the book. Virginia Greene, Lynn Grant, and Julia Lawson of the Conservation Lab prepared various pieces for photography, often at short notice, with good grace and their usual expertise.

Other Museum departments contributed as well: the Registrar's Office, in particular Chrisso Boulis; Jack Murray, Scott Thom, and Srimivas Suvvada in the Exhibits Department; and the Facilities Office. The following people provided support of various kinds: Elizabeth Hamilton, Ban Chiang Project; Jean Walker, Egyptian Section; Dr. Erle Leichty, Tonia Sharlach, and Kevin Danti, Babylonian Section; Laurie Carroll, Asian Section; Maureen Goldsmith, Director's Office; Dr. Stuart Fleming, MASCA; Bethany Engel, Traveling Exhibits; Dr. Lee Horne; Flint Dibble; Jeremy Kucholtz; Rachel Scott; Ayşe Gursan Salzmann; Dr. Nancy S. Steinhardt, Asian and Middle Eastern Studies, University of Pennsylvania; and Dr. Michael W. Meister, South Asia Regional Studies, University of Pennsylvania. Conna Clark, Manager of Rights and Reproductions, and Darielle Mason at the Philadelphia Museum of Art generously donated a photograph of Plate 70.

Finally, I would like to offer thanks to my past and present colleagues in Publications, who got me through the rough patches and cheered me on: Matthew Manieri, Jim Mathieu, Beebe Bahrami, John Walker, and Walda Metcalf.

—JQ